I0031978

The Workbook

COMPANION BOOK TO PARTNERSHIP OR PARTNERSH*T: YOU DECIDE

A CRITICAL TOOL FOR BUILDING A HUMAN FOUNDATION FOR YOUR PARTNERSHIP AND YOUR BUSINESS.

CONCEPT+ WRITING BY PATTY SOFFER
LAYOUT AND DESIGN BY VANESSA FLORES

·AHF·

A HUMAN FOUNDATION PUBLISHING, LLC

The Workbook may be purchased for educational, business or sales promotional use.

For information, please contact A Human Foundation Publishing, 18402 NE 27 Court, Aventura FL 33160

info@ahumanfoundation.com

ISBN   978-0-9859173-4-0 electronic

         978-0-9859173-3-3 paperback

Written by Patty Soffer

Interior design, composition and graphics created by Vanessa Flores, sobe-creative.com

Meet Buster.

This little guy has been conceived in honor of my late father, who inspired me, guided me and taught me to approach life in a simple, loving, midwestern kind of way.

I've put Buster to work guiding you through this very important partnership process because he knew the value of a sense of humor. You'll need one as you build your partnership, company and life.

Dad's life was all about laughter and play. He knew himself inside and out so there was no mistaking what he wanted and didn't want. I hope he inspires these qualities in you too, because this is the very core of your Human Foundation.

So go for it, because in the end, all that will ever matter is whether or not you were happy.

The rest? As dad would say, it's all just sh*t.

Dedicated to my dad, Rolly R. (Buster) Hogue

1921-2009

People, *then business.*

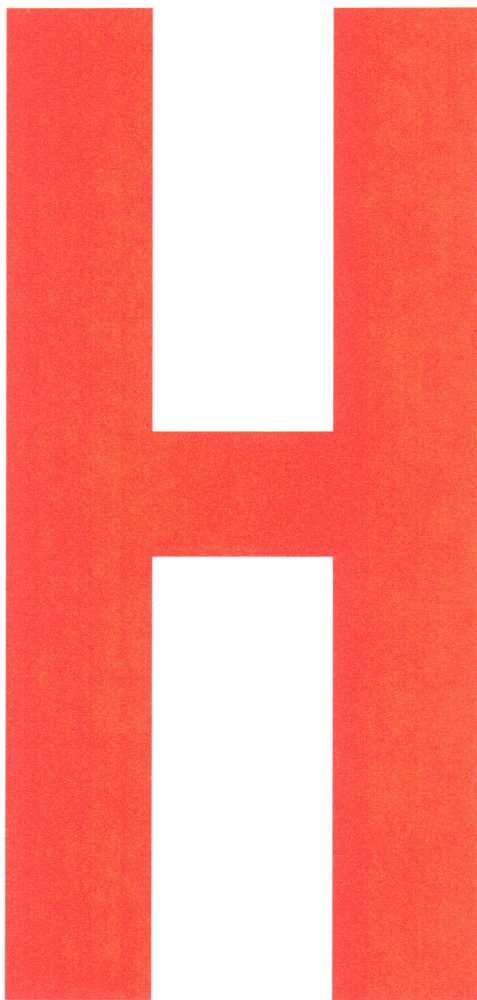

HELLO

So nice to see you!

My name is Buster and I will be your guide.

Ready to build something wonderful?

Let's do this!

ABOUT THE WORKBOOK

Ok we're gonna take a **wild** guess here.

If you have purchased **The Workbook** and the accompanying *Partnership or Partnersh*t: You Decide* book, you are either:

A. Just starting a new business and have zero idea what Partnersh*t even is.

B. Already buried in Partnersh*t.

C. The smartest dude on the planet because you're building your Partnership first, and then your Business.

Way to go

C's

You are starting at the Real Beginning

- Before you commit to a partner
- Before you order the logo-and-a-website special
- Before you buy or lease equipment and office space
- Before you write the business plan
- Before you write the branding and marketing plans
- Before you look for financing
- Before you hire anyone
- Before you start the hunt for clients

Most people are not C's.

So they end up buried knee-deep in **Partnersh*t** before they know it.

For all you 's out there

Let's stop any problems before they start by:

- Getting to know yourself
- Declaring who you are and what you want
- Exploring the ins and outs of partnerships
- Deciding if partnership is right for you
- Deciding what kind of partnership is right for you
- Knowing how to choose a partner who suits you
- Doing the work necessary for becoming a good partner
- Setting the partner-biz mission, vision and goals
- Creating an atmosphere of open communication
- Understanding that partnerships need attention every day
- Knowing how to manage your partnership
- Learning from and about your partnership
- Planning an exit strategy
- Realizing when it's time to move on

And **B**'s

You need to **STOP EVERYTHING** and do this work:

- Before your anger gets the best of you

- Before you put your health and finances at risk

- Before you call the lawyers

- Before you hurt yourself and others

- Before you spend more money

- **Before you destroy absolutely everything you worked so hard to achieve**

HOW TO USE THIS WORKBOOK

1.

Read *Partnersh*t or Partnersh*t: You Decide* so you understand the philosophy behind Building a Human Foundation. The book is is filled with guidance and case studies so you can understand what the questions mean.

You can order it at **www.partnersht.com**

2.

Take our FREE Partnersh*t Detector Quiz. Go to **www.ahumanfoundation.com** and select either **New** or **Existing** Partnerships. The quizzes will let you know immediately where the danger zones are in your partnership and what you are missing.

3.

Go to our home page at
www.ahumanfoundation.com
to book an appointment for your
Partnership Consultation. We will
review your quiz results
and give you guidance. We will
also review options for helping
you completing the **Partnersh*t 2
Partnership (P2P) Process.**

4.★

The Options:

a. **The Do-It-Yourself Option**

b. **The Hybrid Option**

c. **The Up Close and Personal Option**

All three options are explained in detail at

www.ahumanfoundation.com/detailed-consultation

5.

The **Workbook** has been set up for two
partners. If there are more than two, you
can download free extra worksheets at

www.ahumanfoundation.com/downloads

SECTIONS 1 THRU 5

help you
Build Your Human Foundation.

a. There are no redundant questions, even though it seems there are. Trust the Process.

b. Do not make any final partnership decision until you have completed Sections 1-5.

c. Understand that conflicts are not deal breakers nor are they all bad.

d. Conflict can make a partnership better if managed properly.

e. Sometimes you can turn conflicts into business assets.

1

Allocate 3 days of 5 hours each of uninterrupted time together for Sections 1-5.

    a. The Process is by no means fast (think about how long you date before you get married. Ok, it's not that long, but it requires the same explorations), but it is critical to your success. Give it the time and attention it deserves.

2

Answer each question in the space provided in The **Workbook**, starting on page 38. Write your answers privately. No talking and no cheating. These have to be **your** answers, straight from your heart. There are no right or wrong answers. Say what you feel. You will live by what you say so get it all out there into the open.

3

Do one section at a time. No skipping around.

4

Once you finish writing your answers in The **Workbook**, your moderator will ask you that section's questions and you will answer out loud, as will your partner.

    a.   Be sure to also write your partner's answers in the space allotted in The**Workbook**.

    b.   Your moderator will write your answers on giant easel sticky notes so you can easily see any patterns.

    c.   At this time, each question is open for discussion. Remember not to make anyone wrong. Again, there are no right or wrong answers.

    d.   You are looking for areas of compatibility and conflict. Then you will discuss compromise.

5

At the end cf each chapter, there is a recap section. Fill this out before you go on to the next section.

In the end you want to have recorded each partner's answers to all the questions so you can refer back when it comes time to create your Partnership Plan. The template is on page 198.

NOW TAKE ⭐ BREAK

THIS MIGHT BE AS SHORT AS A FEW DAYS

AND AS LONG AS A COUPLE OF WEEKS, SO YOU CAN DIGEST EVERYTHING YOU HAVE DISCUSSED.

YOU WILL KNOW AT THIS POINT WHETHER YOU HAVE WHAT IT TAKES TO BUILD A GOOD PARTNERSHIP. IF IT'S A "YES," BRAVO! YOU'VE BUILT A HUMAN FOUNDATION! YOU'RE STRONG AND READY TO MOVE ON TO THE NEXT SECTIONS, WHICH WILL FOCUS ON BUILDING THE BUSINESS.

IF IT'S "NO," THAT'S COOL TOO. BE HAPPY YOU'RE MAKING AN INFORMED DECISION THAT WILL SAVE YOU FROM AN ABSOLUTE SH*TSTORM OF TROUBLE LATER ON.

Once you've created your Human Foundation, it's time to have some fun

SECTIONS 6 AND 7

help you build your business and brand.

This is where most companies start:
they do all the visual and business stuff first.

And that is why they run into trouble.

They are doing things backwards.

The proper way to build your business is from your Human Foundation up:

MARKETINGSTRATEGY
BRANDINGSTRATEGY
BUSINESS STRATEGY
OSTERWALDER'S
—BUSINESS MODEL CANVAS PROCESS—
A**HUMAN**FOUNDATION
—VIA THE PAR+NERSHIP -TO-PARTNERSH*T PROCESS—

We are huge fans of Osterwalder's Business Model Canvas (BMC) and now is the time to use it.

You can work with the sample BMC in this book on page 176 or go to
www.businessmodelgeneration.com/canvas
and download as many as you need.
While you're at it, we highly recommend you order their books.

This BMC tool will be your best friend.
Use it to build a business or even a project.

You'll thank us! (and Osterwalder's.)

1.

Complete the Business Model Canvas.
Allocate a day to do this and a few days to review and revise.

2.

Create your Business Strategy
Much will become apparent on the BMC. A good friend to have at this point is the Kauffman Foundation **(www. kauffman.org).** They exist for entrepreneurs and offer mountains of free guidance. Look, listen and learn.

3.

Create your Brand Strategy.
This section requires the services of a branding and design company, but we'll provide you with important information so you are aware and ready. Brand development is the face of your brand; how you look, feel, sound and promise. Do not take any silly shortcuts after you have done all this fabulous Human Foundation and Business Building.

4.

Create your Marketing Strategy.
Here, too, we will give you some general information. This is a companion to your brand strategy and is part of the branding experience.

Once you get to

SECTION
8

it's time to create your
Partnership Plan.
Some partners choose to do this after they
complete the first 5 steps;
others wait until the end.

What is important is that you do it.

CREATE YOUR PARTNERSHIP PLAN

You will find a template
on page 196 or you can go to
www.ahumanfoundation.com/downloads

YOU MIGHT BE WONDERING HOW YOU'LL KNOW
IF YOU ARE HEADED FOR PARTNERSH*T?

BY
TAKING
OUR
FREE
PARTNERSH*T
DETECTOR
QUIZZES

14 SYMPTOMS OF PARTNERSH*T

- YOU TALK ABOUT EACH OTHER BEHIND BACKS
- YOU LOSE RESPECT FOR EACH OTHER
- YOU ENLIST ALLIES AND CREATE FACTIONS
- YOU CAN'T SLEEP
- YOU LOSE FOCUS
- YOU STOP LISTENING TO EACH OTHER
- YOU STOP HAVING FUN
- YOUR SELF-RESPECT DISAPPEARS
- YOU STOP TALKING TO EACH OTHER
- YOUR BUSINESS BEGINS TO SUFFER
- YOUR PASSION WANES
- YOU STOP EATING (OR EAT EVERYTHING IN TOWN)
- YOUR CREATIVITY DIPS
- YOU START MAKING EMOTIONAL, NOT BUSINESS, DECISIONS

THE PARTNERSH*T
DETECTOR
QUIZZES HELP YOU

ASK
YOURSELF
SOME PRETTY IMPORTANT QUESTIONS

- ☐ I am happy with my partner right now.
- ☐ I am happy with myself right now.
- ☐ My partnership is fulfilling to me.
- ☐ I feel very supported by my partner.
- ☐ My job strengths live up to my job title.
- ☐ My partner's strengths live up to his/her job title.
- ☐ Our partnership is smooth right now, with no friction.
- ☐ I am scared or concerned about my partner or partnership.
- ☐ My partner and I are able to speak freely and openly with each other.
- ☐ I am a good listener.
- ☐ My partner is a good listener.
- ☐ I am accountable for everything I do, no matter what it is.
- ☐ My partner and I keep our partnership business private and between just us.
- ☐ We have a clear and defined structure in place for regular meetings with each other.
- ☐ We have a set agenda for regular meetings that include the following topics:
    - ☐ a) How's business?
    - ☐ b) Are we where we want to be?
    - ☐ c) Are we achieving our goals?
    - ☐ d) What's not working?
- ☐ We have clear and defined methods in place for managing partner conflicts.
- ☐ Our employees are happy and fulfilled.
- ☐ Business is good right now.
- ☐ I believe the partnership is at least partially responsible for business being good right now.
- ☐ I know exactly why I want a partner/partnership.

You'll find the quizzes on our homepage at **ahumanfoundation.com**
You will get your results by email, along with a link to a ton of valuable information.

If you get stuck or don't understand something, refer to your textbook or poke around the website. Both are rich in case studies, examples and other info.

When you are ready, start Building your Human Foundation on the next pages.

OK,
ARE
YOU
EXCITED?
IT'S
TIME
TO
BUILD
YOUR
HUMAN
FOUNDATION

BUILD YOUR HUMAN FOUNDATION

STEP

1

WHO ARE YOU UNDER THE HOOD?

CHARACTERIZATION

Who are you? What motivates you? Partnership starts with you, so let's talk nakedly about your personal goals, desires, thoughts, values, ideals and filters. This creates a baseline of your "why," the most important thing you must know. Your "why" is your motivation.

1 Why are you here, doing this process?

YOUR ANSWER

YOUR PARTNER'S ANSWER

COMPATIBILITIES

CONFLICTS

DISCUSSION | NOTES

COMPROMISES MADE

2   What is important about answer #1?

YOUR ANSWER

_____
_____
_____
_____
_____
_____
_____
_____
_____
_____
_____

YOUR PARTNER'S ANSWER

_____
_____
_____
_____
_____
_____
_____
_____
_____
_____
_____

COMPATIBILITIES	CONFLICTS

DISCUSSION I NOTES	COMPROMISES MADE

3

Look at answers 1 and 2. What will having those things do for you?
This answer will tell you what your filter is.

YOUR ANSWER

YOUR PARTNER'S ANSWER

COMPATIBILITIES	CONFLICTS

DISCUSSION I NOTES	COMPROMISES MADE

4

What is your intention and what outcome do you wish to achieve by completing this process?

YOUR ANSWER

YOUR PARTNER'S ANSWER

COMPATIBILITIES

CONFLICTS

DISCUSSION | NOTES

COMPROMISES MADE

5

Will achieving this intention and outcome satisfy you?

YOUR ANSWER

YOUR PARTNER'S ANSWER

COMPATIBILITIES

CONFLICTS

DISCUSSION | NOTES

COMPROMISES MADE

6 Are you a left-brain factual or right-brain imaginative?

YOUR ANSWER

_____
_____
_____
_____
_____
_____
_____
_____
_____
_____
_____
_____

YOUR PARTNER'S ANSWER

_____
_____
_____
_____
_____
_____
_____
_____
_____
_____
_____
_____

COMPATIBILITIES

CONFLICTS

DISCUSSION I NOTES

COMPROMISES MADE

7

Are you an introvert, extrovert or a little of both?

YOUR ANSWER

YOUR PARTNER'S ANSWER

COMPATIBILITIES

CONFLICTS

DISCUSSION | NOTES

COMPROMISES MADE

8

Are you Ready. Aim. Fire. or Ready. Fire. Aim.?

YOUR ANSWER

_____
_____
_____
_____
_____
_____
_____
_____
_____
_____
_____
_____
_____

YOUR PARTNER'S ANSWER

_____
_____
_____
_____
_____
_____
_____
_____
_____
_____
_____
_____
_____

COMPATIBILITIES	CONFLICTS

DISCUSSION I NOTES	COMPROMISES MADE

9

Would you describe your personality/drive (NOT your sexual identity) as dominant masculine or dominant feminine?

YOUR ANSWER

YOUR PARTNER'S ANSWER

COMPATIBILITIES

CONFLICTS

DISCUSSION | NOTES

COMPROMISES MADE

10   **Are you Batman or Robin?**

YOUR ANSWER

YOUR PARTNER'S ANSWER

COMPATIBILITIES

CONFLICTS

DISCUSSION | NOTES

COMPROMISES MADE

11

What feeds you? (accomplishment, giving, travel, money, possessions, people, learning, etc.)

YOUR ANSWER

YOUR PARTNER'S ANSWER

COMPATIBILITIES

CONFLICTS

DISCUSSION | NOTES

COMPROMISES MADE

12

What limits you? (fear, laziness, lack of focus, unavailability, obligation, etc.)

YOUR ANSWER

YOUR PARTNER'S ANSWER

COMPATIBILITIES

CONFLICTS

DISCUSSION I NOTES

COMPROMISES MADE

13 What makes you angry?

YOUR ANSWER

YOUR PARTNER'S ANSWER

COMPATIBILITIES

CONFLICTS

DISCUSSION | NOTES

COMPROMISES MADE

14

What is your best quality?

YOUR ANSWER

YOUR PARTNER'S ANSWER

COMPATIBILITIES

CONFLICTS

DISCUSSION | NOTES

COMPROMISES MADE

15 What is your greatest strength?

YOUR ANSWER

YOUR PARTNER'S ANSWER

COMPATIBILITIES	CONFLICTS

DISCUSSION I NOTES	COMPROMISES MADE

16

What is your absolute worst quality?

YOUR ANSWER

_____
_____
_____
_____
_____
_____
_____
_____
_____
_____
_____
_____

YOUR PARTNER'S ANSWER

_____
_____
_____
_____
_____
_____
_____
_____
_____
_____
_____
_____

COMPATIBILITIES

CONFLICTS

DISCUSSION | NOTES

COMPROMISES MADE

17 **What is your greatest weakness?**

YOUR ANSWER

YOUR PARTNER'S ANSWER

COMPATIBILITIES

CONFLICTS

DISCUSSION I NOTES

COMPROMISES MADE

18 What will you absolutely not tolerate under any circumstances?

YOUR ANSWER

_____
_____
_____
_____
_____
_____
_____
_____
_____
_____
_____
_____

YOUR PARTNER'S ANSWER

_____
_____
_____
_____
_____
_____
_____
_____
_____
_____
_____
_____

COMPATIBILITIES

CONFLICTS

DISCUSSION | NOTES

COMPROMISES MADE

19

What do you absolutely refuse to do?

YOUR ANSWER

YOUR PARTNER'S ANSWER

COMPATIBILITIES

CONFLICTS

DISCUSSION | NOTES

COMPROMISES MADE

20

List the 10 most important things/emotions/areas that you value in your life.

YOUR ANSWER

YOUR PARTNER'S ANSWER

COMPATIBILITIES

CONFLICTS

DISCUSSION | NOTES

COMPROMISES MADE

21

Where and how do you get energy? Will this business/partnership feed or support that?

YOUR ANSWER

YOUR PARTNER'S ANSWER

COMPATIBILITIES

CONFLICTS

DISCUSSION | NOTES

COMPROMISES MADE

22

In the spirit of "Baby Shoes" by Ernest Hemingway, write a captivating tale of who you are in exactly six words.

YOUR ANSWER

YOUR PARTNER'S ANSWER

COMPATIBILITIES

CONFLICTS

DISCUSSION | NOTES

COMPROMISES MADE

23

Do you think your partner sees you this way?

YOUR ANSWER

YOUR PARTNER'S ANSWER

COMPATIBILITIES

CONFLICTS

DISCUSSION | NOTES

COMPROMISES MADE

24

What are you grateful for?

YOUR ANSWER

YOUR PARTNER'S ANSWER

COMPATIBILITIES

CONFLICTS

DISCUSSION I NOTES

COMPROMISES MADE

Recap Grid: Use this grid to indicate the areas of compatibility, conflict and compromise. Use blue for compatibility, red for conflict and yellow for compromise. You will quickly see what you need to work on.

1. Why are you here?
2. What is important about answer #1?
3. What is your filter?
4. What is your intention/outcome?
5. Will achieving intention/outcome satisfy you?
6. Left brained?
6. Right brained?
7. Introvert?
7. Extrovert?
7. Ambivert
8. Ready. Aim. Fire.?
8. Ready. Fire. Aim.?
9. Dominant masculine energy?
9. Dominant feminine energy?
10. Batman?
10. Robin?
11. What feeds you?
12. What limits you?
13. What makes you angry?
14. Your best quality?
15. Greatest strength?
16. Absolute worst quality?
17. Greatest weakness?
18. Will not tolerate?
19. Refuse to do?
20. 10 most important values?
21. Where/how do you get energy?
22. Baby shoes/ who you are?
23. Does your partner see you this way?
24. What are you grateful for?

TOTALS

COMPATIBILITY		CONFLICTS		COMPROMISES	
Partner 1	Partner 2	Partner 1	Partner 2	Partner 1	Partner 2

NOTES

BUILD YOUR HUMAN FOUNDATION

STEP

IT'S YOU AND ME, KID

COLLABORATION

How do you approach partnership and business? How does each fit into your life? What are your skills, strengths, weaknesses, expectations and offerings?

1

Define "Partnership."

YOUR ANSWER

YOUR PARTNER'S ANSWER

COMPATIBILITIES

CONFLICTS

DISCUSSION | NOTES

COMPROMISES MADE

2

Is your definition compatible with that of your partner?

YOUR ANSWER

YOUR PARTNER'S ANSWER

COMPATIBILITIES	CONFLICTS

DISCUSSION	NOTES	COMPROMISES MADE

3

Why do you want a partner?

YOUR ANSWER

_____
_____
_____
_____
_____
_____
_____
_____
_____
_____
_____

YOUR PARTNER'S ANSWER

_____
_____
_____
_____
_____
_____
_____
_____
_____
_____
_____

COMPATIBILITIES	CONFLICTS

DISCUSSION I NOTES	COMPROMISES MADE

4   Is there another way you could work together without being partners?

YOUR ANSWER

YOUR PARTNER'S ANSWER

COMPATIBILITIES

CONFLICTS

DISCUSSION | NOTES

COMPROMISES MADE

5

What are the most important qualities are you looking for in a partner? (honesty, skill, financial strength, etc.)

YOUR ANSWER

YOUR PARTNER'S ANSWER

COMPATIBILITIES	CONFLICTS

DISCUSSION I NOTES	COMPROMISES MADE

6

Describe the perfect day in your life.

YOUR ANSWER

YOUR PARTNER'S ANSWER

COMPATIBILITIES

CONFLICTS

DISCUSSION | NOTES

COMPROMISES MADE

7

Will this partnership and business feed that?

YOUR ANSWER

YOUR PARTNER'S ANSWER

COMPATIBILITIES

CONFLICTS

DISCUSSION I NOTES

COMPROMISES MADE

8   **How do you envision your lifestyle as a result of this partnership/business?**

YOUR ANSWER

_____
_____
_____
_____
_____
_____
_____
_____
_____
_____
_____
_____

YOUR PARTNER'S ANSWER

_____
_____
_____
_____
_____
_____
_____
_____
_____
_____
_____
_____

COMPATIBILITIES

CONFLICTS

DISCUSSION I NOTES

COMPROMISES MADE

9

Is it substantially different from what it is now? How?

YOUR ANSWER

_____
_____
_____
_____
_____
_____
_____
_____
_____
_____
_____

YOUR PARTNER'S ANSWER

_____
_____
_____
_____
_____
_____
_____
_____
_____
_____
_____

COMPATIBILITIES

CONFLICTS

DISCUSSION I NOTES

COMPROMISES MADE

10

What does a typical workday look like to you? Define specifically.

YOUR ANSWER

YOUR PARTNER'S ANSWER

COMPATIBILITIES

CONFLICTS

DISCUSSION | NOTES

COMPROMISES MADE

11 Is it important that your partner has the same definition?

YOUR ANSWER

YOUR PARTNER'S ANSWER

COMPATIBILITIES

CONFLICTS

DISCUSSION I NOTES

COMPROMISES MADE

12

What are you good or great at, both tangible and intangible? (e.g., typing, negotiation, bookkeeping, schmoozing, etc.)

YOUR ANSWER

YOUR PARTNER'S ANSWER

COMPATIBILITIES

CONFLICTS

DISCUSSION | NOTES

COMPROMISES MADE

13

What are you bad at, both tangible and intangible?

YOUR ANSWER

YOUR PARTNER'S ANSWER

COMPATIBILITIES

CONFLICTS

DISCUSSION | NOTES

COMPROMISES MADE

14

What specific skills and talents will our business need?

YOUR ANSWER

YOUR PARTNER'S ANSWER

COMPATIBILITIES

CONFLICTS

DISCUSSION | NOTES

COMPROMISES MADE

15

What skills and talents are missing from this partnership?

YOUR ANSWER

YOUR PARTNER'S ANSWER

COMPATIBILITIES

CONFLICTS

DISCUSSION I NOTES

COMPROMISES MADE

16

What will your title be?

YOUR ANSWER

YOUR PARTNER'S ANSWER

COMPATIBILITIES

CONFLICTS

DISCUSSION | NOTES

COMPROMISES MADE

17

Do your skills, talents and strengths live up to your title?

YOUR ANSWER

YOUR PARTNER'S ANSWER

COMPATIBILITIES

CONFLICTS

DISCUSSION | NOTES

COMPROMISES MADE

18

Write your job description. Be very detailed and clear.

YOUR ANSWER	YOUR PARTNER'S ANSWER

COMPATIBILITIES	CONFLICTS

DISCUSSION I NOTES	COMPROMISES MADE

19

What scares or concerns you about your partner or this partnership? Why?

YOUR ANSWER

YOUR PARTNER'S ANSWER

COMPATIBILITIES

CONFLICTS

DISCUSSION | NOTES

COMPROMISES MADE

20

What excites you about your partner or this partnership? Why?

YOUR ANSWER

YOUR PARTNER'S ANSWER

COMPATIBILITIES

CONFLICTS

DISCUSSION | NOTES

COMPROMISES MADE

21   What do you expect from your partner?

YOUR ANSWER

YOUR PARTNER'S ANSWER

COMPATIBILITIES	CONFLICTS

DISCUSSION	NOTES	COMPROMISES MADE

22 What can your partner expect from you?

YOUR ANSWER

YOUR PARTNER'S ANSWER

COMPATIBILITIES

CONFLICTS

DISCUSSION | NOTES

COMPROMISES MADE

23

What expectations do you have of yourself?

YOUR ANSWER

_____
_____
_____
_____
_____
_____
_____
_____
_____
_____
_____
_____

YOUR PARTNER'S ANSWER

_____
_____
_____
_____
_____
_____
_____
_____
_____
_____
_____
_____

COMPATIBILITIES	CONFLICTS

DISCUSSION I NOTES	COMPROMISES MADE

24

What do you like the most about your partner? Why?

YOUR ANSWER

YOUR PARTNER'S ANSWER

COMPATIBILITIES

CONFLICTS

DISCUSSION | NOTES

COMPROMISES MADE

25

Now define Partnership again. Has your definition changed since you started this section?

YOUR ANSWER

_____
_____
_____
_____
_____
_____
_____
_____
_____
_____
_____

YOUR PARTNER'S ANSWER

_____
_____
_____
_____
_____
_____
_____
_____
_____
_____
_____

COMPATIBILITIES	CONFLICTS

DISCUSSION | NOTES	COMPROMISES MADE

Recap Grid: Use this grid to indicate the areas of compatibility, conflict and compromise. Use blue for compatibility, red for conflict and yellow for compromise. You will quickly see what you need to work on.

1. Define partnership.
2. Is the definition compatible with your partner's?
3. Why do you want a partner?
4. Another way you could work together?
5. Most important qualities you're looking for?
6. Perfect day in your life?
7. Will the partnership and business feed that?
8. How do you envision lifestyle as result of partnership?
9. Substantially different than it is now?
10. Typical workday for you?
11. Important that you partner have the same definition?
12. What are you good/great at?
13. What are you bad at?
14. What skills and talents will the business need?
15. What skills and talents are missing?
16. What will your title be?
17. Do your skills/talents live up to your title?
18. What is your job description?
19. What scares/concerns you?
20. What excites you?
21. What do you expect from your partner?
22. What can your partner expect from you?
24. What do you most like about your partner?

TOTALS

COMPATIBILITY		CONFLICTS		COMPROMISES	
Partner 1	Partner 2	Partner 1	Partner 2	Partner 1	Partner 2

NOTES

BUILD YOUR HUMAN FOUNDATION

STEP

3

LET'S SHARE!

COMMUNICATION

What's your language? Verbal? Nonverbal? Witty? Sarcastic? Loud? Quiet? It all matters. Don't force people to have to guess who you are. Claim it and let the world know you're standing by it.

1

What is your communication style? (loud, funny, quiet, electronic, face-to-face, etc.)

YOUR ANSWER

YOUR PARTNER'S ANSWER

COMPATIBILITIES	CONFLICTS

DISCUSSION I NOTES	COMPROMISES MADE

2

What is your personal style? (corporate, hippie, cautious, carefree, etc.)

YOUR ANSWER

_____
_____
_____
_____
_____
_____
_____
_____
_____
_____
_____
_____

YOUR PARTNER'S ANSWER

_____
_____
_____
_____
_____
_____
_____
_____
_____
_____
_____
_____

COMPATIBILITIES

CONFLICTS

DISCUSSION | NOTES

COMPROMISES MADE

3

How do you best express yourself? (writing, singing, speaking, poetry, nonverbal, dance, etc.)

YOUR ANSWER

YOUR PARTNER'S ANSWER

COMPATIBILITIES

CONFLICTS

DISCUSSION I NOTES

COMPROMISES MADE

4

What kind of communication don't you like? (face-to-face, phone, texting, etc.)

YOUR ANSWER

YOUR PARTNER'S ANSWER

COMPATIBILITIES

CONFLICTS

DISCUSSION | NOTES

COMPROMISES MADE

5

What makes you happy?

YOUR ANSWER

_____

YOUR PARTNER'S ANSWER

_____

COMPATIBILITIES

CONFLICTS

DISCUSSION I NOTES

COMPROMISES MADE

6

What shuts you down? (crying, loudness, fighting, etc.)

YOUR ANSWER

YOUR PARTNER'S ANSWER

COMPATIBILITIES	CONFLICTS

DISCUSSION I NOTES	COMPROMISES MADE

7

What is your dominant mood? (serious, happy, sad, pensive, silly, etc.)

YOUR ANSWER

YOUR PARTNER'S ANSWER

COMPATIBILITIES

CONFLICTS

DISCUSSION I NOTES

COMPROMISES MADE

8

What bothers you? (noise, tardiness, sloppiness, etc.)

YOUR ANSWER

YOUR PARTNER'S ANSWER

| COMPATIBILITIES | CONFLICTS |

| DISCUSSION I NOTES | COMPROMISES MADE |

9

How do you communicate when you're under stress or in a crisis?

YOUR ANSWER

YOUR PARTNER'S ANSWER

COMPATIBILITIES	CONFLICTS

DISCUSSION I NOTES	COMPROMISES MADE

10

How do you release stress?

YOUR ANSWER

YOUR PARTNER'S ANSWER

COMPATIBILITIES	CONFLICTS

DISCUSSION	NOTES	COMPROMISES MADE

11

In a crowded room, do you stand out or stand outside?

YOUR ANSWER

YOUR PARTNER'S ANSWER

COMPATIBILITIES

CONFLICTS

DISCUSSION | NOTES

COMPROMISES MADE

12

How do you solve day-to-day problems?

YOUR ANSWER

YOUR PARTNER'S ANSWER

COMPATIBILITIES

CONFLICTS

DISCUSSION | NOTES

COMPROMISES MADE

13 Now define Partnership again. Any changes since you started this section?

YOUR ANSWER

YOUR PARTNER'S ANSWER

COMPATIBILITIES

CONFLICTS

DISCUSSION I NOTES

COMPROMISES MADE

Recap Grid: Use this grid to indicate the areas of compatibility, conflict and compromise. Use blue for compatibility, red for conflict and yellow for compromise. You will quickly see what you need to work on.

1. Communication style?
2. Personal style?
3. How do you best express yourself?
4. What kind of communication don't you like?
5. What makes you happy?
6. What shuts you down?
7. What is your dominant mood?
8. What bothers you?
9. How do you communicate under stress/in a crisis?
10. How do you release stress?
11. I stand out.
11. I stand alone.
12. How do you solve day-to-day problems?

TOTALS

COMPATIBILITY		CONFLICTS		COMPROMISES	
Partner 1	Partner 2	Partner 1	Partner 2	Partner 1	Partner 2

NOTES

STEP

4

TELL ME WHAT YOU WANT
WHAT YOU REALLY REALLY WANT

COMPENSATION

What do you want? Do you even know? This section helps you answer this most important question.

1 Why do you want this business?

YOUR ANSWER

_____
_____
_____
_____
_____
_____
_____
_____
_____
_____
_____
_____

YOUR PARTNER'S ANSWER

_____
_____
_____
_____
_____
_____
_____
_____
_____
_____
_____
_____

COMPATIBILITIES	CONFLICTS

DISCUSSION I NOTES	COMPROMISES MADE

2

What exactly do you want from this business? (power, belonging, money, stature, a platform, a big office, lots of toys, etc.)

YOUR ANSWER

YOUR PARTNER'S ANSWER

COMPATIBILITIES

CONFLICTS

DISCUSSION | NOTES

COMPROMISES MADE

3

Which best describes you: Mission driven, Vision driven, or Profit driven?

YOUR ANSWER

_____
_____
_____
_____
_____
_____
_____
_____
_____
_____
_____

YOUR PARTNER'S ANSWER

_____
_____
_____
_____
_____
_____
_____
_____
_____
_____
_____

COMPATIBILITIES	CONFLICTS

DISCUSSION I NOTES	COMPROMISES MADE

4

What exactly does ownership mean to you? (equal split, strategic partner, investor, etc.)

YOUR ANSWER

YOUR PARTNER'S ANSWER

COMPATIBILITIES

CONFLICTS

DISCUSSION | NOTES

COMPROMISES MADE

5 What exactly does money mean to you? (freedom, power, stature, ability to give, etc.)

YOUR ANSWER

YOUR PARTNER'S ANSWER

COMPATIBILITIES

CONFLICTS

DISCUSSION | NOTES

COMPROMISES MADE

6

What is your money style? (Spend? Save? Invest?)

YOUR ANSWER

YOUR PARTNER'S ANSWER

COMPATIBILITIES

CONFLICTS

DISCUSSION | NOTES

COMPROMISES MADE

7

Do you see your business as a savings vehicle or a cash machine?

YOUR ANSWER

YOUR PARTNER'S ANSWER

COMPATIBILITIES

CONFLICTS

DISCUSSION | NOTES

COMPROMISES MADE

8 **Are you investing any money in this business/partnership? If so, what?**

YOUR ANSWER

YOUR PARTNER'S ANSWER

| COMPATIBILITIES | CONFLICTS |

| DISCUSSION | NOTES | COMPROMISES MADE |

9

Are you investing any intellectual or other property in this business/partnership? If so, what?

YOUR ANSWER

YOUR PARTNER'S ANSWER

COMPATIBILITIES

CONFLICTS

DISCUSSION | NOTES

COMPROMISES MADE

10

How will you value that (those) investment(s)?

YOUR ANSWER

YOUR PARTNER'S ANSWER

COMPATIBILITIES

CONFLICTS

DISCUSSION | NOTES

COMPROMISES MADE

11

How will you recoup that (those) investment(s)?

YOUR ANSWER

YOUR PARTNER'S ANSWER

COMPATIBILITIES

CONFLICTS

DISCUSSION I NOTES

COMPROMISES MADE

12

What financial compensation do you want from this business? Please be specific about amounts, bonuses, draws, etc.

YOUR ANSWER

YOUR PARTNER'S ANSWER

COMPATIBILITIES

CONFLICTS

DISCUSSION | NOTES

COMPROMISES MADE

13

Have you ever filed bankruptcy? If so, why? How was it resolved? Will you document this to an uninvolved third-party professional for verification?

YOUR ANSWER

YOUR PARTNER'S ANSWER

COMPATIBILITIES

CONFLICTS

DISCUSSION | NOTES

COMPROMISES MADE

14

How is your credit? What is your credit score? Will you document this number to an uninvolved third-party professional for verification?

YOUR ANSWER

YOUR PARTNER'S ANSWER

COMPATIBILITIES

CONFLICTS

DISCUSSION | NOTES

COMPROMISES MADE

15

Are you willing to have an uninvolved third-party professional review and confirm your financial statement and /or credit application on all potential partnership bank loans?

YOUR ANSWER

YOUR PARTNER'S ANSWER

COMPATIBILITIES

CONFLICTS

DISCUSSION | NOTES

COMPROMISES MADE

16

Are you willing to purchase life insurance on your potential partner and not cash it in without the other person's knowledge and permission?

YOUR ANSWER

YOUR PARTNER'S ANSWER

COMPATIBILITIES

CONFLICTS

DISCUSSION | NOTES

COMPROMISES MADE

17

Is there anything in your past or present life that could potentially affect this partnership? (illness, legal issues, addiction, financial trouble, incarceration, etc.)

YOUR ANSWER

YOUR PARTNER'S ANSWER

COMPATIBILITIES	CONFLICTS

DISCUSSION	NOTES	COMPROMISES MADE

18

Define "Success."

YOUR ANSWER

_____

_____

_____

_____

_____

_____

_____

_____

_____

_____

_____

YOUR PARTNER'S ANSWER

_____

_____

_____

_____

_____

_____

_____

_____

_____

_____

_____

COMPATIBILITIES	CONFLICTS

DISCUSSION | NOTES	COMPROMISES MADE

19

Define "Failure."

YOUR ANSWER

_____
_____
_____
_____
_____
_____
_____
_____
_____
_____
_____

YOUR PARTNER'S ANSWER

_____
_____
_____
_____
_____
_____
_____
_____
_____
_____
_____

COMPATIBILITIES

CONFLICTS

DISCUSSION | NOTES

COMPROMISES MADE

20

How long can you maintain your interest and participation in this business while it struggles to become profitable?

YOUR ANSWER

YOUR PARTNER'S ANSWER

COMPATIBILITIES

CONFLICTS

DISCUSSION | NOTES

COMPROMISES MADE

21

How do you feel about involving family members in the business?

YOUR ANSWER

_____
_____
_____
_____
_____
_____
_____
_____
_____
_____
_____
_____

YOUR PARTNER'S ANSWER

_____
_____
_____
_____
_____
_____
_____
_____
_____
_____
_____
_____

COMPATIBILITIES

CONFLICTS

DISCUSSION I NOTES

COMPROMISES MADE

22

Do you intend to involve any family members in this business? If so, who, in what positions, and at what compensation package?

YOUR ANSWER

YOUR PARTNER'S ANSWER

COMPATIBILITIES

CONFLICTS

DISCUSSION | NOTES

COMPROMISES MADE

23

What's your 10-year life plan?

YOUR ANSWER

YOUR PARTNER'S ANSWER

COMPATIBILITIES

CONFLICTS

DISCUSSION I NOTES

COMPROMISES MADE

24

How do you envision this partnership ending? (leave and sell to partner, split and close, selling, merger, etc.)

YOUR ANSWER

YOUR PARTNER'S ANSWER

COMPATIBILITIES

CONFLICTS

DISCUSSION | NOTES

COMPROMISES MADE

25

Are you willing to create an exit strategy?

YOUR ANSWER

YOUR PARTNER'S ANSWER

COMPATIBILITIES	CONFLICTS

DISCUSSION	NOTES	COMPROMISES MADE

Recap Grid: Use this grid to indicate the areas of compatibility, conflict and compromise. Use blue for compatibility, red for conflict and yellow for compromise. You will quickly see what you need to work on.

	COMPATIBILITY		CONFLICTS		COMPROMISES	
	Partner 1	Partner 2	Partner 1	Partner 2	Partner 1	Partner 2
1. Why do you want this business?						
2. What do you want from this business?						
3. Mission Driven?						
3. Vision Driven?						
3. Profit Driven?						
4. Ownership split?						
5. What does money mean to you?						
6. Money style-Spend?						
6. Money style-Save?						
6. Money style-Invest?						
7. Business is savings vehicle?						
7. Business is cash machine?						
8. Investing any money in the business?						
9. Investing intellectual or other property in the business?						
10. How will you value those investments?						
11. How will you recoup those investments?						
12. Financial compensation?						
13. Ever file bankruptcy?						
14. Credit score good.						
14. Credit score fair.						
14. Credit score poor.						
15. Willing to have financial statement reviewed by 3rd party?						
16. Willing to purchase life insurance naming partner as beneficiary?						
17. Any ghosts in the closet?						
18. Definition of success?						
19. Definition of failure?						
20. How long can you go until company becomes profitable?						
21. How do you feel about hiring the family?						
22. Which family members are you hiring and at what cost?						
23. 10-year life plan?						
24. How does this partnership end?						
25. Willing to create an exit strategy?						

TOTALS

NOTES

STEP

5

.

YOU GOTTA GIVE TO GET

CONTRIBUTION

Here's a twist on an old expression: Them that gives, gets. Contribution is a mindset. Is it yours? It's okay if it's not, unless you have a partner who lives and breathes contribution. Then you have a problem. Dig in and discover.

1

What does "giving back" mean to you?

YOUR ANSWER

YOUR PARTNER'S ANSWER

COMPATIBILITIES

CONFLICTS

DISCUSSION | NOTES

COMPROMISES MADE

2

Do you believe in giving back? Why or why not?

YOUR ANSWER

YOUR PARTNER'S ANSWER

COMPATIBILITIES

CONFLICTS

DISCUSSION | NOTES

COMPROMISES MADE

3

Is it important that your partner be philanthropic? Why or why not?

YOUR ANSWER

YOUR PARTNER'S ANSWER

COMPATIBILITIES	CONFLICTS

DISCUSSION I NOTES	COMPROMISES MADE

4   **Is it important that your company be philanthropic? Why or why not?**

YOUR ANSWER

YOUR PARTNER'S ANSWER

COMPATIBILITIES

CONFLICTS

DISCUSSION I NOTES

COMPROMISES MADE

5

Would you support college or other intern programs? Why or why not?

YOUR ANSWER

YOUR PARTNER'S ANSWER

COMPATIBILITIES	CONFLICTS

DISCUSSION	NOTES	COMPROMISES MADE

6

Would you sponsor a potential employee for a green card? Why or why not?

YOUR ANSWER

YOUR PARTNER'S ANSWER

COMPATIBILITIES

CONFLICTS

DISCUSSION I NOTES

COMPROMISES MADE

7

Would you be willing to donate some of your business income to a worthy cause? Why or why not?

YOUR ANSWER

_____
_____
_____
_____
_____
_____
_____
_____
_____
_____
_____

YOUR PARTNER'S ANSWER

_____
_____
_____
_____
_____
_____
_____
_____
_____
_____
_____

COMPATIBILITIES	CONFLICTS

DISCUSSION I NOTES	COMPROMISES MADE

8

What causes, entities, or efforts would you be willing for the business to support, with donations of either time or money?

YOUR ANSWER

YOUR PARTNER'S ANSWER

COMPATIBILITIES

CONFLICTS

DISCUSSION | NOTES

COMPROMISES MADE

149

9

Write a one-sentence statement about contribution.

YOUR ANSWER

YOUR PARTNER'S ANSWER

COMPATIBILITIES

CONFLICTS

DISCUSSION I NOTES

COMPROMISES MADE

10

Now define Partnership again. Has it changed since you started this section?

YOUR ANSWER

YOUR PARTNER'S ANSWER

COMPATIBILITIES	CONFLICTS

DISCUSSION	NOTES	COMPROMISES MADE

Recap Grid: Use this grid to indicate the areas of compatibility, conflict and compromise. Use blue for compatibility, red for conflict and yellow for compromise. You will quickly see what you need to work on.

1. What does giving back mean to you?
2. Do you believe in giving back?
3. Important that your partner is philanthropic?
4. Important that your company be philanthropic?
5. Support college or other intern programs?
6. Sponsor for a Green Card?
7. Willing to donate % of company income?
8. Any specific causes you would be willing for company to support?
8. Donate time?
9. Donate money?
10. Contribution Statement

TOTALS

COMPATIBILITY		CONFLICTS		COMPROMISES	
Partner 1	Partner 2	Partner 1	Partner 2	Partner 1	Partner 2

NOTES

STEP

6

BUILD, BABY, BUILD!

CONSTRUCTION

It's time for tangible, strategic thoughts. Dollar-making ideas. Goals, outcomes and measurement criteria. You get to build the business YOU want. How cool is that?

1

What business are you in?

YOUR ANSWER

YOUR PARTNER'S ANSWER

COMPATIBILITIES

CONFLICTS

DISCUSSION | NOTES

COMPROMISES MADE

2

Why are you in this business?

YOUR ANSWER

_____
_____
_____
_____
_____
_____
_____
_____
_____
_____
_____

YOUR PARTNER'S ANSWER

_____
_____
_____
_____
_____
_____
_____
_____
_____
_____
_____

COMPATIBILITIES

CONFLICTS

DISCUSSION I NOTES

COMPROMISES MADE

3

Does this business or the idea of this business fulfill your expectations/desires? Why or why not?

YOUR ANSWER

_____

_____

_____

_____

_____

_____

_____

_____

_____

_____

_____

YOUR PARTNER'S ANSWER

_____

_____

_____

_____

_____

_____

_____

_____

_____

_____

_____

COMPATIBILITIES	CONFLICTS

DISCUSSION I NOTES	COMPROMISES MADE

4

Is there anything lacking in this business that might take your interest away from it? If so, what?

YOUR ANSWER

YOUR PARTNER'S ANSWER

COMPATIBILITIES	CONFLICTS

DISCUSSION	NOTES	COMPROMISES MADE

5

Describe your vision for the business in one sentence.

YOUR ANSWER

YOUR PARTNER'S ANSWER

COMPATIBILITIES	CONFLICTS

DISCUSSION	NOTES	COMPROMISES MADE

6

What is the mission of your business?

YOUR ANSWER

_____

_____

_____

_____

_____

_____

_____

_____

_____

_____

_____

_____

YOUR PARTNER'S ANSWER

_____

_____

_____

_____

_____

_____

_____

_____

_____

_____

_____

_____

COMPATIBILITIES	CONFLICTS

DISCUSSION I NOTES	COMPROMISES MADE

7

Write your Onliness Statement*. You are the only company that . . . .
*Developed by Marty Neumeier, ZAG

YOUR ANSWER

WHAT

HOW

WHO

WHERE

WHY

WHEN

YOUR PARTNER'S ANSWER

WHAT

HOW

WHO

WHERE

WHY

WHEN

COMPATIBILITIES	CONFLICTS

DISCUSSION I NOTES	COMPROMISES MADE

8

What are your three most important goals for the next year?

YOUR ANSWER

YOUR PARTNER'S ANSWER

COMPATIBILITIES

CONFLICTS

DISCUSSION | NOTES

COMPROMISES MADE

9

What are those goals dependent upon? What has to happen to achieve those goals?

YOUR ANSWER

YOUR PARTNER'S ANSWER

COMPATIBILITIES	CONFLICTS

DISCUSSION I NOTES	COMPROMISES MADE

10

Look ahead to the future and write a scenario incorporating your most fervent wishes for this business.

YOUR ANSWER

YOUR PARTNER'S ANSWER

COMPATIBILITIES

CONFLICTS

DISCUSSION I NOTES

COMPROMISES MADE

11   How soon will this happen?

YOUR ANSWER

_____

_____

_____

_____

_____

_____

_____

_____

_____

_____

_____

YOUR PARTNER'S ANSWER

_____

_____

_____

_____

_____

_____

_____

_____

_____

_____

_____

COMPATIBILITIES	CONFLICTS

DISCUSSION I NOTES	COMPROMISES MADE

12

Look ahead to the future and write a scenario incorporating the worst that could happen in this business.

YOUR ANSWER

YOUR PARTNER'S ANSWER

COMPATIBILITIES

CONFLICTS

DISCUSSION I NOTES

COMPROMISES MADE

13

What would you do or how far would you go to avoid having that scenario ever happen?

YOUR ANSWER

YOUR PARTNER'S ANSWER

COMPATIBILITIES

CONFLICTS

DISCUSSION | NOTES

COMPROMISES MADE

Recap Grid: Use this grid to indicate the areas of compatibility, conflict and compromise. Use blue for compatibility, red for conflict and yellow for compromise. You will quickly see what you need to work on.

1. What business are you in?
2. Why are you in this business?
3. Does this business or the idea of this business fulfill your expectations/ desires? Why or why not?
4. Is there anything lacking in this business that might take your interest away from it? If so, what?
5. Describe your vision for the business in one sentence.
6. What is the mission of your business?
7. Write your Onliness Statement
8. What are your three most important goals for the next year?
9. What are those goals dependent upon? What has to happen to achieve those goals?
10. Look ahead to the future and write a scenario incorporating your most fervent wishes for this business.
11. How soon will this happen?
12. Look ahead to the future and write a scenario incorporating the worst that could happen in this business.
13. What would you do or how far would you go to avoid having that scenario ever happen?

TOTALS

COMPATIBILITY		CONFLICTS		COMPROMISES	
Partner 1	Partner 2	Partner 1	Partner 2	Partner 1	Partner 2

NOTES

STEP

7

LOOKIN' GOOD!

CREATION

This sections contains general information, advice and links to some fabulous resources to help you create your Business Model Canvas; Brand Strategy, Marketing Strategy.

BUSINESS MODEL CANVAS

.com

How would you like to create your business on one sheet of paper?

Business Model Canvas (BMC) is the best tool we have found to zoom in on exactly what you do, offer, want, have, need, who your customers are, how you will get the word out, where the money is and what all this will cost.

In this era of short attention spans, believe us: BMC is a secret weapon that will render those long, boring business reports obsolete. (Nobody read them anyway).

You can use BMC to strategize a business, a project, a partnership, a personal brand or even a great dinner party.

We are raving fans of Business Model Canvas. Go to **businessmodelcanvas.com** and see for yourself. You can download it. Or, just turn the page. It's there. Use it.

Next, every entrepreneur should also become friendly with The Kauffman Foundation. They are in existence for one reason: to serve entrepreneurs. It is a gold mine of resources, information and downloads on nearly every topic relevant to business and beyond.

www.kauffman.org/

THE BUSINESS MODEL CANVAS

Designed for:

KEY PARTNERS	KEY ACTIVITIES	VALUE PROPOSITIONS
	KEY RESOURCES	

CUSTOMER RELATIONSHIPS

CUSTOMER SEGMENTS

REVENUE STREAMS

BRAND
STRATEGY
GUIDE

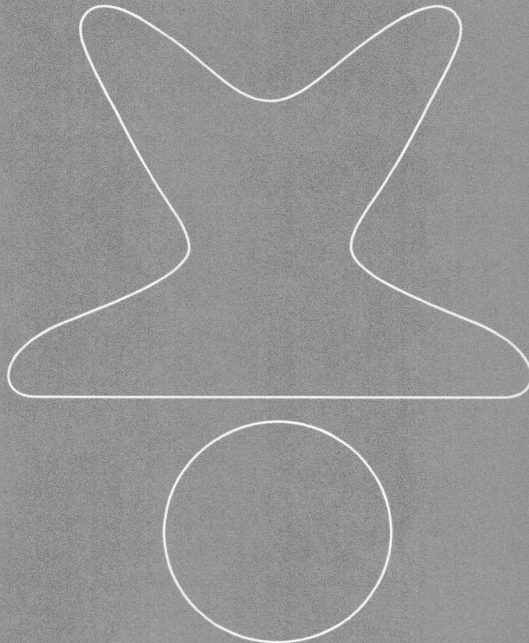

Branding is creating an identity.

Branding is an art and, developed properly, a tremendous business asset.

We recommend you work with a professional
branding agency for this section.

Use this framework as a guide. Because Branding does not lend itself to a
Workbook format, we are providing you with general guidelines. Your
branding agency will have a preferred method, but in the end, these are
the general steps you will go through.

A. Research Phase

Some of this will sound familiar because we covered it in Step #6: Construction. Because you have completed the P2P Process, you already have quite a head start. Here's a recap:

- Who are you
- What business are you in
- Your mission and vision
- Your strengths and weaknesses
- Your key stakeholders
- Your product(s)
- Your target market
- Your competition
- Your competitive advantage
- How you will organize your company
- Your office/ corporate culture
- Near-and long-term goals

B. Strategic and Clarification Phase

Think rationally, analytically and creatively. See what's up out there in the world. Where do your customers live? How do they buy? To answer these questions, you will need to:

1. **Understand your Brand**
   a. What is your marketing strategy?
   b. What are the general industry, cultural and political trends.
   c. How will you price your product?
   d. How will you distribute?

2. **Voice your Brand**
   a. Create your Brand Brief
      This document solidifies the understanding of your brand.
   b. Create your Creative Brief
      This is your brand road map and will keep you focused and on track as you develop creative.

3. **Name your Brand**
   Your company's name is an asset, as are employees, clients, products and fixtures. Naming is a process like everything else. Give it its due.

In this phase, you will do the following:

1. Create your color palette.

- Effective use of color is a science. Colors elicit emotions, memories, associations and behaviors from people. Make sure what you choose represents the goals you have in mind.

2. Define tyopgraphy

- Type is to branding as water is to life.

3. Create the logo/symbol

- This graphic representation of your company's name is your anchor. People think in pictures first, and your logo will root them to your brand—good or bad.

4. Define the voice for video and audio.

- It's a new age. Video and audio are it. Websites are video-driven today, and many products, especially service-oriented products,are downloaded or sold as DVDs. Pay sharp attention to both the message and the messenger.

5. Test.

- What you create must work across the brand. The logo must be scalable; appropriate for all media including and especially the web; legible at all sizes; adaptable in color and black/white; accommodative of cultural differences.

D. Development Phase

Protect your brand and hard work via trademarking (™), service marking (SM), or copywriting (©). You can do this online via www.uspto.gov and www.copyright.gov, www.Legalzoom.com or call your attorney for assistance. It's also time to create the brand extensions. The possibilities are virtually endless and dependent upon the business you are in, but here are some of the more common branded items:

- Letterhead Set
- Business Card
- Website
- Apps
- Web Favicons
- Brochures or other printed collateral
- Signage
- Product Packaging
- Ads
- Environmental Graphics
- Uniforms
- Other stuff called "Ephemera"

E. Management Phase

Like anything else, your brand requires tender loving care. It's a living, breathing entity that will grow and change over time. What do you stand for? What did you promise? Why did you attract the customers in the first place? How is your retention? What are the complaints? Your customers will come back time and again if you live up to your promises, make them feel like kings, stay ahead with innovation and deliver a consistent experience.

The type of business you are in will determine your measurement categories and they are typically defined by your CFO.

- Cash flow
- Customer behavior
- Market Share
- Loyalty
- Revenue per customer
- Sales projections
- Response rates
- Web analytics
- Social media analytics
- Employee performance and retention

Obviously there are things that cannot be "measured" in the acceptable sense but are nonetheless critical to a brand's success or failure. Some of these are:

- Perception
- Pride
- Public Relations
- Satisfaction
- Sustainability
- Community Standing

MARKETING STRATEGY GUIDE

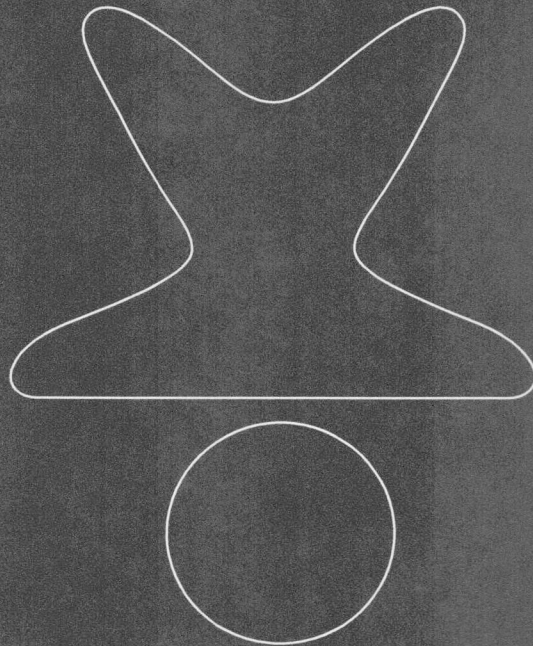

Marketing is managing the promise of your brand.

Marketing is the core of your business growth and is all about motivating people to action. The secret doesn't only lie in price; it lies in the value you deliver. Market that value and meet the needs of your customers. Get yourself a great marketing agency or make sure you have a marketing whiz on your team. The best branding in the world will go nowhere unless it is properly marketed, and whomever handles your marketing must understand what motivates people.

Marketing plans are essentially problem/solution documents. You will find many marketing plan outlines. Find one that best suits your business. Our process is to start at the end (outcome/goals) and work backwards and includes the following steps:

1. Defined Outcome/Goals
2. Product Description
3. SWOT
4. Research
    a. Business Environment Analysis
    b. Market Research /Market Segmentation
5. Product Positioning/Marketing Mix
6. Budget
7. Execution
8. Evaluation

The techniques you use will depend upon your product or service. However, many of these are critical no matter what you sell or do. We have starred them because they are the stars in the celestial skies of marketing.

1. Credibility*

Be the expert you say you are. Be the company you say you are. Be consistent, available, trustworthy and always concerned about your customers

2. Concern*

The universe is shifting. People can do business with anyone anywhere. but we are still people, and a true heart connection will win every time.

3. Commonality*

Be relatable to your customers. Walk in their shoes. Make their problem and your solution a collaboration.

4. Framing*

Create an emotional mental picture and choose words that touch people's hearts, not heads. Identify their pain points: what is hurting or scaring them? Then solve in an emotional way.

5. Scarcity

Limited availability creates a desire to buy.

6. Exclusivity

We all want to be a member of the "cool" club, have the Limited Edition whatever or have access to whatever is behind the velvet rope.

7. Challenge

Introduce a challenge to the customer. Then present the solution.

8. Choices

People love options, whether in size, color, payments, etc. Careful not to offer too many options, though. That creates confusion.

9 Humor

People love to laugh. Laughter lightens tension. The rest is whether your product or service resonates.

10. Random Kindness

Do something nice just for the hell of it. Share something special. Give something away. You will get it back in a thousand ways.

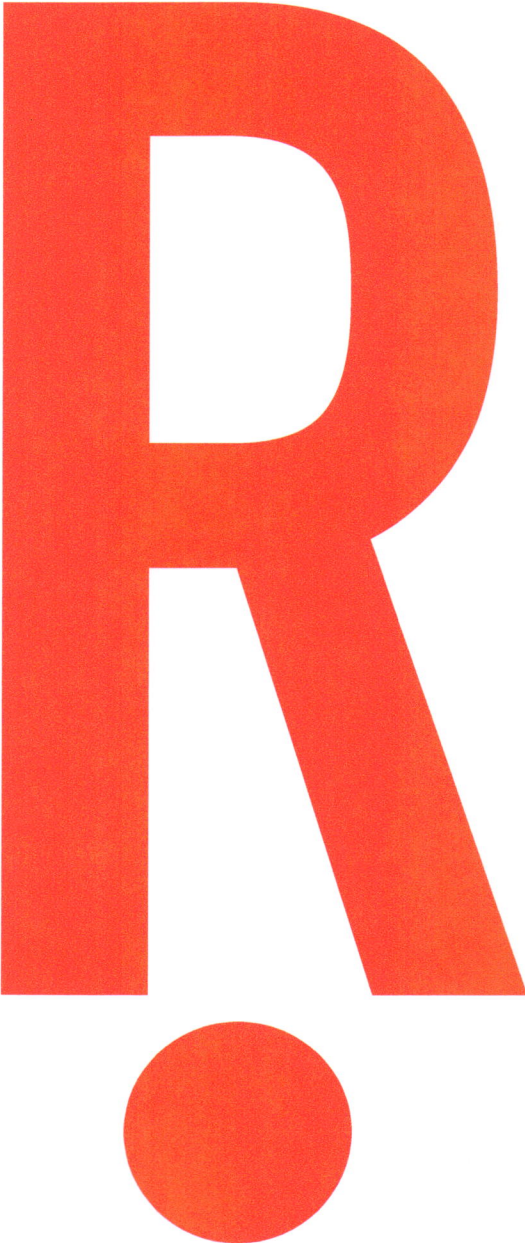

R.

TIME TO WRITE THE PLAN

RESOURCES

One cannot build or create without the proper tools. The P2P process has provided you with the necessary tools to create your partnership and business. Now it's time to harvest all you have learned and let it support and nourish you. Here are some more great tools for that.

INTEGRATION

It's time to reflect. Think about everything you have learned about yourself and your partner. Take some time to journal it on the next pages. Declare yourself. Writing things down keeps them alive and keeps you accountable.

1 My reason(s) for doing this process was/were… Write as much or as little as you want. Just make sure you write from your heart.

_____
_____
_____
_____
_____
_____
_____
_____
_____
_____
_____
_____
_____
_____
_____
_____
_____
_____
_____
_____
_____

2 The 10 keywords that I heard when I LISTENED to my partner speak during this process are:

1. _____
2. _____
3. _____
4. _____
5. _____
6. _____
7. _____
8. _____
9. _____
10. _____

3 The five most important distinctions that I made (about anything) during the P2P Process, in order of importance, are:

1. _____
_____
2. _____
_____
3. _____
_____
4. _____
_____
5. _____
_____

4 To honor those distinctions, I will commit to the following:

1. _____
_____
2. _____
_____
3. _____
_____
4. _____
_____
5. _____
_____

5 The top three things I will commit to so I can passionately empower this partnership are:

1. _____
_____
2. _____
_____
3. _____
_____

6 When we hit a bump, I will…

_____
_____
_____
_____
_____
_____
_____
_____
_____

7 I have learned from and am acknowledging, honoring, respecting and empowering my partner, and myself right here, right now, because…

_____
_____
_____
_____
_____

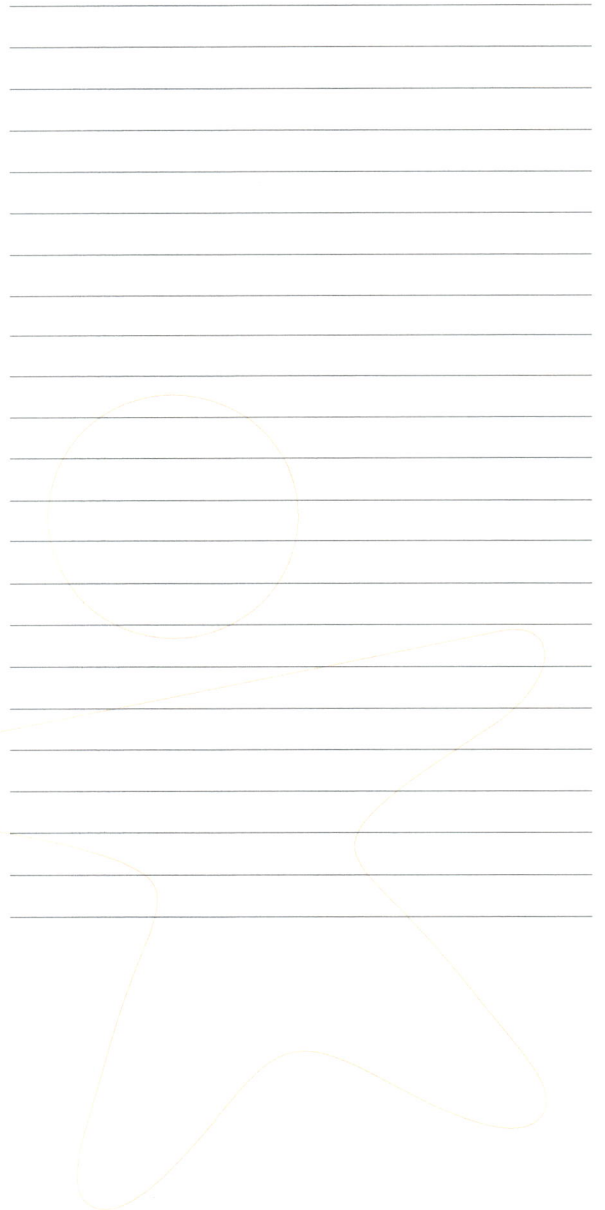

8 Write down anything else that touched you, scared you, pleased you, hurt you or inspired you. To honor those distinctions, I will commit to the following:

1. _____

2. _____

3. _____

4. _____

5. _____

9 The top three things I will commit to so I can passionately empower this partnership are:

1. _____

2. _____

3. _____

NOTES

PARTNERSHIP PLAN TEMPLATE

**THIS TEMPLATE IS INTENDED TO GUIDE YOU AND YOUR PARTNER
IN CREATING YOUR PARTNERSHIP PLAN.**

Every partnership is different, so each agreement will reflect the personalities of and issues relevant to the partners. Because of the differences in partners and types of businesses, there is no real template that can apply to all. Additionally, each state has different laws, and each legal entity is managed differently.

However, please feel free to use this as a guidepost for creating your agreement and be sure to make it your own. This template follows the Partnership 2 Partnership Process featured in ***Partnership or Partnersh*t: You Decide*** and recaps the answers you entered in **The Workbook**.

Your Partnership Plan is your road map that corresponds to the values, goals, accommodations and solutions you established when you built your Human Foundation. Be sure to consult an attorney and financial planner to complete the Compensation section and to review the entire document for any legal red flags.

Because of the nature of this kind of document, it might not be considered a legal document. Check with your attorney. However, it is a moral and ethical document, and carries all the weight and responsibilities thereof.

1. Read Partnership or Partnersh*t: You Decide. How to Build Your Business on the Strongest Foundation There is—A Human Foundation. Available on Amazon.com

2. Complete the Partnersh*t 2 Partnership (P2P) Process contained in Chapters 9-16 in the book.

3. Use **The Workbook** to keep a record of all your answers to all the questions. If you need extra sheets, please download them at ahumanfoundation.com/downloads. Having this permanent record will make creating your Partnership Plan easy.

4. Once you have completed the P2P Process, take a week or two to let everything digest. THIS IS A VERY IMPORTANT STEP.

5. After you have taken some time to think, reconvene with your partner. Each of you needs to then fill out this template. Do this privately and individually. Use as many sheets as necessary. Extras are available at **ahumanfoundation.com/downloads.** The goal is to have everyone write down what is important and what was "sticky" during the process.

6. Compile all answers into one document. See Appendix B in the textbook for examples or download them from **ahumanfoundation.com/downloads**

7. Take your completed Partnership Plan to your attorney and/or financial planner for review. It's important to not let anyone change the agreement if it's what you and your partners want. Rather, your counsel should look for any legal issues that need resolving.

8. Sign the agreement and stand by it. Revisit it at least yearly and be open to any changes and shifts that occur. This is fluid, not static. Just like life.

OUR HUMAN FOUNDATION PARTNERSHIP PLAN

DATE:

NAME OF BUSINESS:

DATE ESTABLISHED:

LEGAL ENTITY:

ADDRESS/PHONE:

OUR VISION:

OUR MISSION:

PARTNER INFORMATION

NAME:

CONTACT INFORMATION:

MY FILTER IS:

WHAT PARTNERSHIP
MEANS TO ME:

JOB TITLE:

JOB DESCRIPTION:

PRECENTAGE OF
OWNERSHIP IN
COMPANY:

NAME:

CONTACT INFORMATION:

MY FILTER IS:

WHAT PARTNERSHIP
MEANS TO ME:

JOB TITLE:

JOB DESCRIPTION:

PRECENTAGE OF
OWNERSHIP IN
COMPANY:

OUR ONLINESS STATEMENT: WHAT MAKES OUR COMPANY UNIQUE *

*Developed by Marty Neumeier, ZAG

WHAT:

HOW:

WHO:

WHERE:

WHY:

WHEN:

CORE VALUE #1

CORE VALUE #2

CORE VALUE #3

CORE VALUE #4

CORE VALUE #5

CORE VALUE #6

CORE VALUE #7

CORE VALUE #8

CORE VALUE #9

CORE VALUE #10

1. CHARACTERIZATION
WHO WE ARE

2. COLLABORATION
HOW WE WILL WORK TOGETHER

4. COMPENSATION
WHAT WE BRING + WHAT WE WANT
(PART A)

COMPANY VALUATION:

WHAT WE BRING	PARTNER 1	PARTNER 2
A. CAPITAL CONTRIBUTION		
CASH		
DELIVERY DATE FOR CONTRIBUTION		
EQUIPMENT		
INTELLECTUAL PROPERTY		
TOTAL VALUE OF CAPITAL CONTRIBUTION		
B. PROFIT / LOSS DISTRIBUTION - PROPORTIONAL		
% OWNERSHIP		
C. PERSONAL EQUITY		

WHAT WE WANT	
PARTNER 1	PARTNER 2

4. COMPENSATION
WHAT WE BRING + WHAT WE WANT
(PART C)

MANAGEMENT

OPERATIONS

TAX AND FINANCIAL MATTERS

CAPITAL CONTRIBUTIONS

NEW PARTNERS AND STOCK
TRANSFER

DISSOLUTION

GENERAL

5. CONTRIBUTION:
WHAT WE GIVE, HOW WE SERVE

6. CONSTRUCTION: HOW WE WILL BUILD

7. CREATION: HOW WE WILL INTERACT WITH THE WORLD

www.ingramcontent.com/pod-product-compliance
Lightning Source LLC
Chambersburg PA
CBHW041950220326
41599CB00004BA/92